A
B

And whatsoever ye do
in word or deed, do all
in the name of the Lord Jesus . . .

Colossians 3:17

Thomas
Kinkade

Name	Home
Address	Work
	Cell
	Pager
Birthday	Fax
E-Mail	

Name	Home
Address	Work
	Cell
	Pager
Birthday	Fax
E-Mail	

Name	Home
Address	Work
	Cell
	Pager
Birthday	Fax
-Mail	

ame	Home
ddress	Work
	Cell
	Pager
rthday	Fax
Mail	

ame	Home
ldress	Work
	Cell
	Pager
thday	Fax
Mail	

me	Home
dress	Work
	Cell
	Pager
hday	Fax
ail	

AB

Name	Home
Address	Work
	Cell
	Pager
Birthday	Fax
E-Mail	

Name	Home
Address	Work
	Cell
	Pager
Birthday	Fax
E-Mail	

Name	Home
Address	Work
	Cell
	Pager
Birthday	Fax
E-Mail	

Name	Home
Address	Work
	Cell
	Pager
Birthday	Fax
E-Mail	

Name	Home
Address	Work
	Cell
	Pager
Birthday	Fax
E-Mail	

Name	Home
Address	Work
	Cell
	Pager
Birthday	Fax
E-Mail	

Name	Home
Address	Work
	Cell
	Pager
Birthday	Fax
E-Mail	

Name	Home
Address	Work
	Cell
	Pager
Birthday	Fax
E-Mail	

Name	Home
Address	Work
	Cell
	Pager
Birthday	Fax
E-Mail	

Name	Home
Address	Work
	Cell
	Pager
Birthday	Fax
E-Mail	

Name	Home
Address	Work
	Cell
	Pager
Birthday	Fax
E-Mail	

Name	Home
Address	Work
	Cell
	Pager
Birthday	Fax
E-Mail	

AB

Name	Home
Address	Work
	Cell
	Pager
Birthday	Fax
E-Mail	

Name	Home
Address	Work
	Cell
	Pager
Birthday	Fax
E-Mail	

Name	Home
Address	Work
	Cell
	Pager
Birthday	Fax
E-Mail	

Name	Home
Address	Work
	Cell
	Pager
Birthday	Fax
E-Mail	

Name	Home
Address	Work
	Cell
	Pager
Birthday	Fax
E-Mail	

Name	Home
Address	Work
	Cell
	Pager
Birthday	Fax
E-Mail	

C
D

*But the path of the just is as
the shining light, that shineth
more and more unto the perfect day.*

Proverbs 4:18

Name	Home
Address	Work
	Cell
	Pager
Birthday	Fax
E-Mail	

Name	Home
Address	Work
	Cell
	Pager
Birthday	Fax
E-Mail	

Name	Home
Address	Work
	Cell
	Pager
Birthday	Fax
E-Mail	

Name	Home
Address	Work
	Cell
	Pager
Birthday	Fax
E-Mail	

Name	Home
Address	Work
	Cell
	Pager
Birthday	Fax
E-Mail	

Name	Home
Address	Work
	Cell
	Pager
Birthday	Fax
E-Mail	

CD

Name		Home
Address		Work
		Cell
		Pager
Birthday		Fax
E-Mail		

Name		Home
Address		Work
		Cell
		Pager
Birthday		Fax
E-Mail		

Name		Home
Address		Work
		Cell
		Pager
Birthday		Fax
E-Mail		

Name		Home
Address		Work
		Cell
		Pager
Birthday		Fax
E-Mail		

Name		Home
Address		Work
		Cell
		Pager
Birthday		Fax
E-Mail		

Name		Home
Address		Work
		Cell
		Pager
Birthday		Fax
E-Mail		

Name	Home
Address	Work
	Cell
	Pager
Birthday	Fax
E-Mail	

Name	Home
Address	Work
	Cell
	Pager
Birthday	Fax
E-Mail	

Name	Home
Address	Work
	Cell
	Pager
Birthday	Fax
E-Mail	

Name	Home
Address	Work
	Cell
	Pager
Birthday	Fax
E-Mail	

Name	Home
Address	Work
	Cell
	Pager
Birthday	Fax
E-Mail	

Name	Home
Address	Work
	Cell
	Pager
Birthday	Fax
E-Mail	

CD

Name	Home
Address	Work
	Cell
	Pager
Birthday	Fax
E-Mail	

Name	Home
Address	Work
	Cell
	Pager
Birthday	Fax
E-Mail	

Name	Home
Address	Work
	Cell
	Pager
Birthday	Fax
E-Mail	

Name	Home
Address	Work
	Cell
	Pager
Birthday	Fax
E-Mail	

Name	Home
Address	Work
	Cell
	Pager
Birthday	Fax
E-Mail	

Name	Home
Address	Work
	Cell
	Pager
Birthday	Fax
E-Mail	

Name	Home
Address	Work
	Cell
	Pager
Birthday	Fax
E-Mail	

Name	Home
Address	Work
	Cell
	Pager
Birthday	Fax
E-Mail	

Name	Home
Address	Work
	Cell
	Pager
Birthday	Fax
E-Mail	

Name	Home
Address	Work
	Cell
	Pager
Birthday	Fax
E-Mail	

Name	Home
Address	Work
	Cell
	Pager
Birthday	Fax
E-Mail	

Name	Home
Address	Work
	Cell
	Pager
Birthday	Fax
E-Mail	

CD

Name	Home
Address	Work
	Cell
	Pager
Birthday	Fax
E-Mail	

Name	Home
Address	Work
	Cell
	Pager
Birthday	Fax
E-Mail	

Name	Home
Address	Work
	Cell
	Pager
Birthday	Fax
E-Mail	

Name	Home
Address	Work
	Cell
	Pager
Birthday	Fax
E-Mail	

Name	Home
Address	Work
	Cell
	Pager
Birthday	Fax
E-Mail	

Name	Home
Address	Work
	Cell
	Pager
Birthday	Fax
E-Mail	

Name	Home
Address	Work
	Cell
	Pager
Birthday	Fax
E-Mail	

Name	Home
Address	Work
	Cell
	Pager
Birthday	Fax
E-Mail	

Name	Home
Address	Work
	Cell
	Pager
Birthday	Fax
E-Mail	

Name	Home
Address	Work
	Cell
	Pager
Birthday	Fax
E-Mail	

Name	Home
Address	Work
	Cell
	Pager
Birthday	Fax
E-Mail	

Name	Home
Address	Work
	Cell
	Pager
Birthday	Fax
E-Mail	

CD

Name	Home
Address	Work
	Cell
	Pager
Birthday	Fax
E-Mail	

Name	Home
Address	Work
	Cell
	Pager
Birthday	Fax
E-Mail	

Name	Home
Address	Work
	Cell
	Pager
Birthday	Fax
E-Mail	

Name	Home
Address	Work
	Cell
	Pager
Birthday	Fax
E-Mail	

Name	Home
Address	Work
	Cell
	Pager
Birthday	Fax
E-Mail	

Name	Home
Address	Work
	Cell
	Pager
Birthday	Fax
E-Mail	

E
F

Be of good comfort,
... be of one mind,
live in peace...

2 Corinthians 13:11

Thomas
Kinkade

EF

Name	Home
Address	Work
	Cell
	Pager
Birthday	Fax
E-Mail	

Name	Home
Address	Work
	Cell
	Pager
Birthday	Fax
E-Mail	

Name	Home
Address	Work
	Cell
	Pager
Birthday	Fax
E-Mail	

Name	Home
Address	Work
	Cell
	Pager
Birthday	Fax
E-Mail	

Name	Home
Address	Work
	Cell
	Pager
Birthday	Fax
E-Mail	

Name	Home
Address	Work
	Cell
	Pager
Birthday	Fax
E-Mail	

Name	Home
Address	Work
	Cell
	Pager
Birthday	Fax
E-Mail	

Name	Home
Address	Work
	Cell
	Pager
Birthday	Fax
E-Mail	

Name	Home
Address	Work
	Cell
	Pager
Birthday	Fax
E-Mail	

Name	Home
Address	Work
	Cell
	Pager
Birthday	Fax
E-Mail	

Name	Home
Address	Work
	Cell
	Pager
Birthday	Fax
E-Mail	

Name	Home
Address	Work
	Cell
	Pager
Birthday	Fax
E-Mail	

Name	Home
Address	Work
	Cell
	Pager
Birthday	Fax
E-Mail	

Name	Home
Address	Work
	Cell
	Pager
Birthday	Fax
E-Mail	

Name	Home
Address	Work
	Cell
	Pager
Birthday	Fax
E-Mail	

Name	Home
Address	Work
	Cell
	Pager
Birthday	Fax
E-Mail	

Name	Home
Address	Work
	Cell
	Pager
Birthday	Fax
E-Mail	

Name	Home
Address	Work
	Cell
	Pager
Birthday	Fax
E-Mail	

EF

Name	Home
Address	Work
	Cell
	Pager
Birthday	Fax
E-Mail	

Name	Home
Address	Work
	Cell
	Pager
Birthday	Fax
E-Mail	

Name	Home
Address	Work
	Cell
	Pager
Birthday	Fax
E-Mail	

Name	Home
Address	Work
	Cell
	Pager
Birthday	Fax
E-Mail	

Name	Home
Address	Work
	Cell
	Pager
Birthday	Fax
E-Mail	

Name	Home
Address	Work
	Cell
	Pager
Birthday	Fax
E-Mail	

Name	Home
Address	Work
	Cell
	Pager
Birthday	Fax
E-Mail	

Name	Home
Address	Work
	Cell
	Pager
Birthday	Fax
E-Mail	

Name	Home
Address	Work
	Cell
	Pager
Birthday	Fax
E-Mail	

Name	Home
Address	Work
	Cell
	Pager
Birthday	Fax
E-Mail	

Name	Home
Address	Work
	Cell
	Pager
Birthday	Fax
E-Mail	

Name	Home
Address	Work
	Cell
	Pager
Birthday	Fax
E-Mail	

EF

Name	Home	
Address	Work	
	Cell	
	Pager	
Birthday	Fax	
E-Mail		

Name	Home	
Address	Work	
	Cell	
	Pager	
Birthday	Fax	
E-Mail		

Name	Home	
Address	Work	
	Cell	
	Pager	
Birthday	Fax	
E-Mail		

Name	Home	
Address	Work	
	Cell	
	Pager	
Birthday	Fax	
E-Mail		

Name	Home	
Address	Work	
	Cell	
	Pager	
Birthday	Fax	
E-Mail		

Name	Home	
Address	Work	
	Cell	
	Pager	
Birthday	Fax	
E-Mail		

Name	Home
Address	Work
	Cell
	Pager
Birthday	Fax
E-Mail	

Name	Home
Address	Work
	Cell
	Pager
Birthday	Fax
E-Mail	

Name	Home
Address	Work
	Cell
	Pager
Birthday	Fax
E-Mail	

Name	Home
Address	Work
	Cell
	Pager
Birthday	Fax
E-Mail	

Name	Home
Address	Work
	Cell
	Pager
Birthday	Fax
E-Mail	

Name	Home
Address	Work
	Cell
	Pager
Birthday	Fax
E-Mail	

EF

Name	Home
Address	Work
	Cell
	Pager
Birthday	Fax
E-Mail	

Name	Home
Address	Work
	Cell
	Pager
Birthday	Fax
E-Mail	

Name	Home
Address	Work
	Cell
	Pager
Birthday	Fax
E-Mail	

Name	Home
Address	Work
	Cell
	Pager
Birthday	Fax
E-Mail	

Name	Home
Address	Work
	Cell
	Pager
Birthday	Fax
E-Mail	

Name	Home
Address	Work
	Cell
	Pager
Birthday	Fax
E-Mail	

Truly the light is sweet, and a pleasant thing it is for the eyes to behold the sun.

Ecclesiastes 11:7

Thomas
Kinkade

Name	Home
Address	Work
	Cell
	Pager
Birthday	Fax
E-Mail	

Name	Home
Address	Work
	Cell
	Pager
Birthday	Fax
E-Mail	

Name	Home
Address	Work
	Cell
	Pager
Birthday	Fax
Mail	

Name	Home
Address	Work
	Cell
	Pager
Birthday	Fax
Mail	

Name	Home
Address	Work
	Cell
	Pager
Birthday	Fax
Mail	

Name	Home
Address	Work
	Cell
	Pager
Birthday	Fax
Mail	

GH

Name	Home
Address	Work
	Cell
	Pager
Birthday	Fax
E-Mail	

Name	Home
Address	Work
	Cell
	Pager
Birthday	Fax
E-Mail	

Name	Home
Address	Work
	Cell
	Pager
Birthday	Fax
E-Mail	

Name	Home
Address	Work
	Cell
	Pager
Birthday	Fax
E-Mail	

Name	Home
Address	Work
	Cell
	Pager
Birthday	Fax
E-Mall	

Name	Home
Address	Work
	Cell
	Pager
Birthday	Fax
E-Mail	

Name	Home
Address	Work
	Cell
	Pager
Birthday	Fax
E-Mail	

Name	Home
Address	Work
	Cell
	Pager
Birthday	Fax
E-Mail	

Name	Home
Address	Work
	Cell
	Pager
Birthday	Fax
Mail	

Name	Home
Address	Work
	Cell
	Pager
Birthday	Fax
Mail	

Name	Home
Address	Work
	Cell
	Pager
Birthday	Fax
Mail	

Name	Home
Address	Work
	Cell
	Pager
Birthday	Fax
Mail	

GH

Name	Home
Address	Work
	Cell
	Pager
Birthday	Fax
E-Mail	

Name	Home
Address	Work
	Cell
	Pager
Birthday	Fax
E-Mail	

Name	Home
Address	Work
	Cell
	Pager
Birthday	Fax
E-Mail	

Name	Home
Address	Work
	Cell
	Pager
Birthday	Fax
E-Mail	

Name	Home
Address	Work
	Cell
	Pager
Birthday	Fax
E-Mail	

Name	Home
Address	Work
	Cell
	Pager
Birthday	Fax
E-Mail	

Name	Home
Address	Work
	Cell
	Pager
Birthday	Fax
E-Mail	

Name	Home
Address	Work
	Cell
	Pager
Birthday	Fax
E-Mail	

Name	Home
Address	Work
	Cell
	Pager
Birthday	Fax
E-Mail	

Name	Home
Address	Work
	Cell
	Pager
Birthday	Fax
E-Mail	

Name	Home
Address	Work
	Cell
	Pager
Birthday	Fax
E-Mail	

Name	Home
Address	Work
	Cell
	Pager
Birthday	Fax
E-Mail	

GH

Name .... Home ....
Address .... Work ....
.... Cell ....
.... Pager ....
Birthday .... Fax ....
E-Mail ....

Name .... Home ....
Address .... Work ....
.... Cell ....
.... Pager ....
Birthday .... Fax ....
E-Mail ....

Name .... Home ....
Address .... Work ....
.... Cell ....
.... Pager ....
Birthday .... Fax ....
E-Mail ....

Name .... Home ....
Address .... Work ....
.... Cell ....
.... Pager ....
Birthday .... Fax ....
E-Mail ....

Name .... Home ....
Address .... Work ....
.... Cell ....
.... Pager ....
Birthday .... Fax ....
E-Mail ....

Name .... Home ....
Address .... Work ....
.... Cell ....
.... Pager ....
Birthday .... Fax ....
E-Mail ....

Name	Home
Address	Work
	Cell
	Pager
Birthday	Fax
E-Mail	

Name	Home
Address	Work
	Cell
	Pager
Birthday	Fax
E-Mail	

Name	Home
Address	Work
	Cell
	Pager
Birthday	Fax
E-Mail	

Name	Home
Address	Work
	Cell
	Pager
Birthday	Fax
E-Mail	

Name	Home
Address	Work
	Cell
	Pager
Birthday	Fax
E-Mail	

Name	Home
Address	Work
	Cell
	Pager
Birthday	Fax
E-Mail	

GH

Name	Home
Address	Work
	Cell
	Pager
Birthday	Fax
E-Mail	

Name	Home
Address	Work
	Cell
	Pager
Birthday	Fax
E-Mail	

Name	Home
Address	Work
	Cell
	Pager
Birthday	Fax
E-Mail	

Name	Home
Address	Work
	Cell
	Pager
Birthday	Fax
E-Mail	

Name	Home
Address	Work
	Cell
	Pager
Birthday	Fax
E-Mail	

Name	Home
Address	Work
	Cell
	Pager
Birthday	Fax
E-Mail	

*And he saith
unto them, Follow me...*

Matthew 4:19

I
J

Thomas
Kinkade

Name	Home
Address	Work
	Cell
	Pager
Birthday	Fax
E-Mail	

Name	Home
Address	Work
	Cell
	Pager
Birthday	Fax
E-Mail	

Name	Home
Address	Work
	Cell
	Pager
Birthday	Fax
E-Mail	

Name	Home
Address	Work
	Cell
	Pager
Birthday	Fax
E-Mail	

Name	Home
Address	Work
	Cell
	Pager
Birthday	Fax
E-Mail	

Name	Home
Address	Work
	Cell
	Pager
Birthday	Fax
E-Mail	

IJ

Name	Home
Address	Work
	Cell
	Pager
Birthday	Fax
E-Mail	

Name	Home
Address	Work
	Cell
	Pager
Birthday	Fax
E-Mail	

Name	Home
Address	Work
	Cell
	Pager
Birthday	Fax
E-Mail	

Name	Home
Address	Work
	Cell
	Pager
Birthday	Fax
E-Mail	

Name	Home
Address	Work
	Cell
	Pager
Birthday	Fax
E-Mail	

Name	Home
Address	Work
	Cell
	Pager
Birthday	Fax
E-Mail	

IJ

Name	Home
Address	Work
	Cell
	Pager
Birthday	Fax
E-Mail	

Name	Home
Address	Work
	Cell
	Pager
Birthday	Fax
E-Mail	

Name	Home
Address	Work
	Cell
	Pager
Birthday	Fax
E-Mail	

Name	Home
Address	Work
	Cell
	Pager
Birthday	Fax
E-Mail	

Name	Home
Address	Work
	Cell
	Pager
Birthday	Fax
E-Mail	

Name	Home
Address	Work
	Cell
	Pager
Birthday	Fax
E-Mail	

IJ

Name	Home
Address	Work
	Cell
	Pager
Birthday	Fax
E-Mail	

Name	Home
Address	Work
	Cell
	Pager
Birthday	Fax
E-Mail	

Name	Home
Address	Work
	Cell
	Pager
Birthday	Fax
E-Mail	

Name	Home
Address	Work
	Cell
	Pager
Birthday	Fax
E-Mail	

Name	Home
Address	Work
	Cell
	Pager
Birthday	Fax
E-Mail	

Name	Home
Address	Work
	Cell
	Pager
Birthday	Fax
E-Mail	

IJ

Name		Home
Address		Work
		Cell
		Pager
Birthday		Fax
E-Mail		

Name		Home
Address		Work
		Cell
		Pager
Birthday		Fax
E-Mail		

Name		Home
Address		Work
		Cell
		Pager
Birthday		Fax
E-Mail		

Name		Home
Address		Work
		Cell
		Pager
Birthday		Fax
E-Mail		

Name		Home
Address		Work
		Cell
		Pager
Birthday		Fax
E-Mail		

Name		Home
Address		Work
		Cell
		Pager
Birthday		Fax
E-Mail		

IJ

Name	Home
Address	Work
	Cell
	Pager
Birthday	Fax
E-Mail	

Name	Home
Address	Work
	Cell
	Pager
Birthday	Fax
E-Mail	

Name	Home
Address	Work
	Cell
	Pager
Birthday	Fax
E-Mail	

Name	Home
Address	Work
	Cell
	Pager
Birthday	Fax
E-Mail	

Name	Home
Address	Work
	Cell
	Pager
Birthday	Fax
F-Mail	

Name	Home
Address	Work
	Cell
	Pager
Birthday	Fax
E-Mail	

Name	Home
Address	Work
	Cell
	Pager
Birthday	Fax
E-Mail	

Name	Home
Address	Work
	Cell
	Pager
Birthday	Fax
E-Mail	

Name	Home
Address	Work
	Cell
	Pager
Birthday	Fax
E-Mail	

Name	Home
Address	Work
	Cell
	Pager
Birthday	Fax
E-Mail	

Name	Home
Address	Work
	Cell
	Pager
Birthday	Fax
E-Mail	

Name	Home
Address	Work
	Cell
	Pager
Birthday	Fax
E-Mail	

IJ

Name	Home
Address	Work
	Cell
	Pager
Birthday	Fax
E-Mail	

Name	Home
Address	Work
	Cell
	Pager
Birthday	Fax
E-Mail	

Name	Home
Address	Work
	Cell
	Pager
Birthday	Fax
E-Mail	

Name	Home
Address	Work
	Cell
	Pager
Birthday	Fax
E-Mail	

Name	Home
Address	Work
	Cell
	Pager
Birthday	Fax
E-Mail	

Name	Home
Address	Work
	Cell
	Pager
Birthday	Fax
E-Mail	

Arise, shine; for thy light is come, and the glory of the LORD is risen upon thee.

Isaiah 60:1

K
L

Name	Home
Address	Work
	Cell
	Pager
Birthday	Fax
E-Mail	

Name	Home
Address	Work
	Cell
	Pager
Birthday	Fax
E-Mail	

Name	Home
Address	Work
	Cell
	Pager
Birthday	Fax
E-Mail	

Name	Home
Address	Work
	Cell
	Pager
Birthday	Fax
E-Mail	

Name	Home
Address	Work
	Cell
	Pager
Birthday	Fax
E-Mail	

Name	Home
Address	Work
	Cell
	Pager
Birthday	Fax
E-Mail	

KL

Name	Home
Address	Work
	Cell
	Pager
Birthday	Fax
E-Mail	

Name	Home
Address	Work
	Cell
	Pager
Birthday	Fax
E-Mail	

Name	Home
Address	Work
	Cell
	Pager
Birthday	Fax
E-Mail	

Name	Home
Address	Work
	Cell
	Pager
Birthday	Fax
E-Mail	

Name	Home
Address	Work
	Cell
	Pager
Birthday	Fax
E-Mail	

Name	Home
Address	Work
	Cell
	Pager
Birthday	Fax
E-Mail	

Name	Home
Address	Work
	Cell
	Pager
Birthday	Fax
E-Mail	

Name	Home
Address	Work
	Cell
	Pager
Birthday	Fax
E-Mail	

Name	Home
Address	Work
	Cell
	Pager
Birthday	Fax
E-Mail	

Name	Home
Address	Work
	Cell
	Pager
Birthday	Fax
E-Mail	

Name	Home
Address	Work
	Cell
	Pager
Birthday	Fax
E-Mail	

Name	Home
Address	Work
	Cell
	Pager
Birthday	Fax
E-Mail	

KL

Name	Home
Address	Work
	Cell
	Pager
Birthday	Fax
E-Mail	

Name	Home
Address	Work
	Cell
	Pager
Birthday	Fax
E-Mail	

Name	Home
Address	Work
	Cell
	Pager
Birthday	Fax
E-Mail	

Name	Home
Address	Work
	Cell
	Pager
Birthday	Fax
E-Mail	

Name	Home
Address	Work
	Cell
	Pager
Birthday	Fax
E-Mail	

Name	Home
Address	Work
	Cell
	Pager
Birthday	Fax
E-Mail	

Name		Home	
Address		Work	
		Cell	
		Pager	
Birthday		Fax	
E-Mail			

Name		Home	
Address		Work	
		Cell	
		Pager	
Birthday		Fax	
E-Mail			

Name		Home	
Address		Work	
		Cell	
		Pager	
Birthday		Fax	
E-Mail			

Name		Home	
Address		Work	
		Cell	
		Pager	
Birthday		Fax	
E-Mail			

Name		Home	
Address		Work	
		Cell	
		Pager	
Birthday		Fax	
E-Mail			

Name		Home	
Address		Work	
		Cell	
		Pager	
Birthday		Fax	
E-Mail			

KL

Name	Home
Address	Work
	Cell
	Pager
Birthday	Fax
E-Mail	

Name	Home
Address	Work
	Cell
	Pager
Birthday	Fax
E-Mail	

Name	Home
Address	Work
	Cell
	Pager
Birthday	Fax
E-Mail	

Name	Home
Address	Work
	Cell
	Pager
Birthday	Fax
E-Mail	

Name	Home
Address	Work
	Cell
	Pager
Birthday	Fax
E-Mail	

Name	Home
Address	Work
	Cell
	Pager
Birthday	Fax
E-Mail	

Name	Home
Address	Work
	Cell
	Pager
Birthday	Fax
E-Mail	

Name	Home
Address	Work
	Cell
	Pager
Birthday	Fax
E-Mail	

Name	Home
Address	Work
	Cell
	Pager
Birthday	Fax
E-Mail	

Name	Home
Address	Work
	Cell
	Pager
Birthday	Fax
E-Mail	

Name	Home
Address	Work
	Cell
	Pager
Birthday	Fax
E-Mail	

Name	Home
Address	Work
	Cell
	Pager
Birthday	Fax
E-Mail	

KL

Name	Home
Address	Work
	Cell
	Pager
Birthday	Fax
E-Mail	

Name	Home
Address	Work
	Cell
	Pager
Birthday	Fax
E-Mail	

Name	Home
Address	Work
	Cell
	Pager
Birthday	Fax
E-Mail	

Name	Home
Address	Work
	Cell
	Pager
Birthday	Fax
E-Mail	

Name	Home
Address	Work
	Cell
	Pager
Birthday	Fax
E-Mail	

Name	Home
Address	Work
	Cell
	Pager
Birthday	Fax
E-Mail	

The LORD *bless thee, and keep thee: The* LORD *make his face shine upon thee . . . and give thee peace.*

Numbers 6:24-26

Thomas Kinkade

Name	Home
Address	Work
	Cell
	Pager
Birthday	Fax
E-Mail	

Name	Home
Address	Work
	Cell
	Pager
Birthday	Fax
E-Mail	

Name	Home
Address	Work
	Cell
	Pager
Birthday	Fax
E-Mail	

Name	Home
Address	Work
	Cell
	Pager
Birthday	Fax
E-Mail	

Name	Home
Address	Work
	Cell
	Pager
Birthday	Fax
E-Mail	

Name	Home
Address	Work
	Cell
	Pager
Birthday	Fax
E-Mail	

MN

Name

Address

Birthday

E-Mail

Home

Work

Cell

Pager

Fax

Name

Address

Birthday

E-Mail

Home

Work

Cell

Pager

Fax

Name

Address

Birthday

E-Mail

Home

Work

Cell

Pager

Fax

Name

Address

Birthday

E-Mail

Home

Work

Cell

Pager

Fax

Name

Address

Birthday

E-Mail

Home

Work

Cell

Pager

Fax

Name

Address

Birthday

E-Mail

Home

Work

Cell

Pager

Fax

MN

Name
Address

Birthday
E-Mail

Home
Work
Cell
Pager
Fax

Name
Address

Birthday
E-Mail

Home
Work
Cell
Pager
Fax

Name
Address

Birthday
E-Mail

Home
Work
Cell
Pager
Fax

Name
Address

Birthday
E-Mail

Home
Work
Cell
Pager
Fax

Name
Address

Birthday
E-Mail

Home
Work
Cell
Pager
Fax

Name
Address

Birthday
E-Mail

Home
Work
Cell
Pager
Fax

MN

Name

Address

Birthday

E-Mail

Home

Work

Cell

Pager

Fax

Name

Address

Birthday

E-Mail

Home

Work

Cell

Pager

Fax

Name

Address

Birthday

E-Mail

Home

Work

Cell

Pager

Fax

Name

Address

Birthday

E-Mail

Home

Work

Cell

Pager

Fax

Name

Address

Birthday

E-Mail

Home

Work

Cell

Pager

Fax

Name

Address

Birthday

E-Mail

Home

Work

Cell

Pager

Fax

Name	Home
Address	Work
	Cell
	Pager
Birthday	Fax
E-Mail	

Name	Home
Address	Work
	Cell
	Pager
Birthday	Fax
E-Mail	

Name	Home
Address	Work
	Cell
	Pager
Birthday	Fax
E-Mail	

Name	Home
Address	Work
	Cell
	Pager
Birthday	Fax
E-Mail	

Name	Home
Address	Work
	Cell
	Pager
Birthday	Fax
E-Mail	

Name	Home
Address	Work
	Cell
	Pager
Birthday	Fax
E-Mail	

MN

Name	Home
Address	Work
	Cell
	Pager
Birthday	Fax
E-Mail	

Name	Home
Address	Work
	Cell
	Pager
Birthday	Fax
E-Mail	

Name	Home
Address	Work
	Cell
	Pager
Birthday	Fax
E-Mail	

Name	Home
Address	Work
	Cell
	Pager
Birthday	Fax
E-Mail	

Name	Home
Address	Work
	Cell
	Pager
Birthday	Fax
E-Mail	

Name	Home
Address	Work
	Cell
	Pager
Birthday	Fax
E-Mail	

Name	Home
Address	Work
	Cell
	Pager
Birthday	Fax
E-Mail	

Name	Home
Address	Work
	Cell
	Pager
Birthday	Fax
E-Mail	

Name	Home
Address	Work
	Cell
	Pager
Birthday	Fax
E-Mail	

Name	Home
Address	Work
	Cell
	Pager
Birthday	Fax
E-Mail	

Name	Home
Address	Work
	Cell
	Pager
Birthday	Fax
E-Mail	

Name	Home
Address	Work
	Cell
	Pager
Birthday	Fax
E-Mail	

MN

Name	Home
Address	Work
	Cell
	Pager
Birthday	Fax
E-Mail	

Name	Home
Address	Work
	Cell
	Pager
Birthday	Fax
E-Mail	

Name	Home
Address	Work
	Cell
	Pager
Birthday	Fax
E-Mail	

Name	Home
Address	Work
	Cell
	Pager
Birthday	Fax
E-Mail	

Name	Home
Address	Work
	Cell
	Pager
Birthday	Fax
E-Mail	

Name	Home
Address	Work
	Cell
	Pager
Birthday	Fax
E-Mail	

*D*elight thyself also in the LORD; and he shall give thee the desires of thine heart.

Psalm 37:4

Thomas Kinkade

Name	Home
Address	Work
	Cell
	Pager
Birthday	Fax
E-Mail	

Name	Home
Address	Work
	Cell
	Pager
Birthday	Fax
E-Mail	

Name	Home
Address	Work
	Cell
	Pager
Birthday	Fax
E-Mail	

Name	Home
Address	Work
	Cell
	Pager
Birthday	Fax
E-Mail	

Name	Home
Address	Work
	Cell
	Pager
Birthday	Fax
E-Mail	

Name	Home
Address	Work
	Cell
	Pager
Birthday	Fax
E-Mail	

OP

Name	Home
Address	Work
	Cell
	Pager
Birthday	Fax
E-Mail	

Name	Home
Address	Work
	Cell
	Pager
Birthday	Fax
E-Mail	

Name	Home
Address	Work
	Cell
	Pager
Birthday	Fax
E-Mail	

Name	Home
Address	Work
	Cell
	Pager
Birthday	Fax
E-Mail	

Name	Home
Address	Work
	Cell
	Pager
Birthday	Fax
E-Mail	

Name	Home
Address	Work
	Cell
	Pager
Birthday	Fax
E-Mail	

OP

Name	Home
Address	Work
	Cell
	Pager
Birthday	Fax
E-Mail	

Name	Home
Address	Work
	Cell
	Pager
Birthday	Fax
E-Mail	

Name	Home
Address	Work
	Cell
	Pager
Birthday	Fax
E-Mail	

Name	Home
Address	Work
	Cell
	Pager
Birthday	Fax
E-Mail	

Name	Home
Address	Work
	Cell
	Pager
Birthday	Fax
E-Mail	

Name	Home
Address	Work
	Cell
	Pager
Birthday	Fax
E-Mail	

OP

Name	Home
Address	Work
	Cell
	Pager
Birthday	Fax
E-Mail	

Name	Home
Address	Work
	Cell
	Pager
Birthday	Fax
E-Mail	

Name	Home
Address	Work
	Cell
	Pager
Birthday	Fax
E-Mail	

Name	Home
Address	Work
	Cell
	Pager
Birthday	Fax
E-Mail	

Name	Home
Address	Work
	Cell
	Pager
Birthday	Fax
E-Mail	

Name	Home
Address	Work
	Cell
	Pager
Birthday	Fax
E-Mail	

Name	Home
Address	Work
	Cell
	Pager
Birthday	Fax
E-Mail	

Name	Home
Address	Work
	Cell
	Pager
Birthday	Fax
E-Mail	

Name	Home
Address	Work
	Cell
	Pager
Birthday	Fax
E-Mail	

Name	Home
Address	Work
	Cell
	Pager
Birthday	Fax
E-Mail	

Name	Home
Address	Work
	Cell
	Pager
Birthday	Fax
E-Mail	

Name	Home
Address	Work
	Cell
	Pager
Birthday	Fax
E-Mail	

OP

Name

Home

Address

Work

Cell

Pager

Birthday

Fax

E-Mail

Name

Home

Address

Work

Cell

Pager

Birthday

Fax

E-Mail

Name

Home

Address

Work

Cell

Pager

Birthday

Fax

E-Mail

Name

Home

Address

Work

Cell

Pager

Birthday

Fax

E-Mail

Name

Home

Address

Work

Cell

Pager

Birthday

Fax

E-Mail

Name

Home

Address

Work

Cell

Pager

Birthday

Fax

E-Mail

OP

Name	Home
Address	Work
	Cell
	Pager
Birthday	Fax
E-Mail	

Name	Home
Address	Work
	Cell
	Pager
Birthday	Fax
E-Mail	

Name	Home
Address	Work
	Cell
	Pager
Birthday	Fax
E-Mail	

Name	Home
Address	Work
	Cell
	Pager
Birthday	Fax
E-Mail	

Name	Home
Address	Work
	Cell
	Pager
Birthday	Fax
E-Mail	

Name	Home
Address	Work
	Cell
	Pager
Birthday	Fax
E-Mail	

OP

Name

Address

Birthday

E-Mail

Home

Work

Cell

Pager

Fax

Name

Address

Birthday

E-Mail

Home

Work

Cell

Pager

Fax

Name

Address

Birthday

E-Mail

Home

Work

Cell

Pager

Fax

Name

Address

Birthday

E-Mail

Home

Work

Cell

Pager

Fax

Name

Address

Birthday

E-Mail

Home

Work

Cell

Pager

Fax

Name

Address

Birthday

E-Mail

Home

Work

Cell

Pager

Fax

Unto thee, O LORD, do I lift up my soul.

Psalm 25:1

Thomas Kinkade

Name	Home
Address	Work
	Cell
	Pager
Birthday	Fax
E-Mail	

Name	Home
Address	Work
	Cell
	Pager
Birthday	Fax
E-Mail	

Name	Home
Address	Work
	Cell
	Pager
Birthday	Fax
E-Mail	

Name	Home
Address	Work
	Cell
	Pager
Birthday	Fax
E-Mail	

Name	Home
Address	Work
	Cell
	Pager
Birthday	Fax
E-Mail	

Name	Home
Address	Work
	Cell
	Pager
Birthday	Fax
E-Mail	

QR

Name	Home
Address	Work
	Cell
	Pager
Birthday	Fax
E-Mail	

Name	Home
Address	Work
	Cell
	Pager
Birthday	Fax
E-Mail	

Name	Home
Address	Work
	Cell
	Pager
Birthday	Fax
E-Mail	

Name	Home
Address	Work
	Cell
	Pager
Birthday	Fax
E-Mail	

Name	Home
Address	Work
	Cell
	Pager
Birthday	Fax
E-Mail	

Name	Home
Address	Work
	Cell
	Pager
Birthday	Fax
E-Mail	

Name	Home
Address	Work
	Cell
	Pager
Birthday	Fax
E-Mail	

Name	Home
Address	Work
	Cell
	Pager
Birthday	Fax
E-Mail	

Name	Home
Address	Work
	Cell
	Pager
Birthday	Fax
E-Mail	

Name	Home
Address	Work
	Cell
	Pager
Birthday	Fax
E-Mail	

Name	Home
Address	Work
	Cell
	Pager
Birthday	Fax
E-Mail	

Name	Home
Address	Work
	Cell
	Pager
Birthday	Fax
E-Mail	

QR

Name	Home
Address	Work
	Cell
	Pager
Birthday	Fax
E-Mail	

Name	Home
Address	Work
	Cell
	Pager
Birthday	Fax
E-Mail	

Name	Home
Address	Work
	Cell
	Pager
Birthday	Fax
E-Mail	

Name	Home
Address	Work
	Cell
	Pager
Birthday	Fax
E-Mail	

Name	Home
Address	Work
	Cell
	Pager
Birthday	Fax
E-Mail	

Name	Home
Address	Work
	Cell
	Pager
Birthday	Fax
E-Mail	

Name	Home
Address	Work
	Cell
	Pager
Birthday	Fax
E-Mail	

Name	Home
Address	Work
	Cell
	Pager
Birthday	Fax
E-Mail	

Name	Home
Address	Work
	Cell
	Pager
Birthday	Fax
E-Mail	

Name	Home
Address	Work
	Cell
	Pager
Birthday	Fax
E-Mail	

Name	Home
Address	Work
	Cell
	Pager
Birthday	Fax
E-Mail	

Name	Home
Address	Work
	Cell
	Pager
Birthday	Fax
E-Mail	

QR

Name	Home
Address	Work
	Cell
	Pager
Birthday	Fax
E-Mail	

Name	Home
Address	Work
	Cell
	Pager
Birthday	Fax
E-Mail	

Name	Home
Address	Work
	Cell
	Pager
Birthday	Fax
E-Mail	

Name	Home
Address	Work
	Cell
	Pager
Birthday	Fax
E-Mail	

Name	Home
Address	Work
	Cell
	Pager
Birthday	Fax
E-Mail	

Name	Home
Address	Work
	Cell
	Pager
Birthday	Fax
E-Mail	

Name	Home
Address	Work
	Cell
	Pager
Birthday	Fax
E-Mail	

Name	Home
Address	Work
	Cell
	Pager
Birthday	Fax
E-Mail	

Name	Home
Address	Work
	Cell
	Pager
Birthday	Fax
E-Mail	

Name	Home
Address	Work
	Cell
	Pager
Birthday	Fax
E-Mail	

Name	Home
Address	Work
	Cell
	Pager
Birthday	Fax
E-Mail	

Name	Home
Address	Work
	Cell
	Pager
Birthday	Fax
E-Mail	

QR

Name	Home
Address	Work
	Cell
	Pager
Birthday	Fax
E-Mail	

Name	Home
Address	Work
	Cell
	Pager
Birthday	Fax
E-Mail	

Name	Home
Address	Work
	Cell
	Pager
Birthday	Fax
E-Mail	

Name	Home
Address	Work
	Cell
	Pager
Birthday	Fax
E-Mail	

Name	Home
Address	Work
	Cell
	Pager
Birthday	Fax
E-Mail	

Name	Home
Address	Work
	Cell
	Pager
Birthday	Fax
E-Mail	

And the fruit of righteousness is sown in peace of them that make peace.

James 3:18

S
T

Thomas Kinkade

Name	Home
Address	Work
	Cell
	Pager
Birthday	Fax
E-Mail	

Name	Home
Address	Work
	Cell
	Pager
Birthday	Fax
E-Mail	

Name	Home
Address	Work
	Cell
	Pager
Birthday	Fax
E-Mail	

Name	Home
Address	Work
	Cell
	Pager
Birthday	Fax
E-Mail	

Name	Home
Address	Work
	Cell
	Pager
Birthday	Fax
E-Mail	

Name	Home
Address	Work
	Cell
	Pager
Birthday	Fax
E-Mail	

ST

Name	Home
Address	Work
	Cell
	Pager
Birthday	Fax
E-Mail	

Name	Home
Address	Work
	Cell
	Pager
Birthday	Fax
E-Mail	

Name	Home
Address	Work
	Cell
	Pager
Birthday	Fax
E-Mail	

Name	Home
Address	Work
	Cell
	Pager
Birthday	Fax
E-Mail	

Name	Home
Address	Work
	Cell
	Pager
Birthday	Fax
E-Mail	

Name	Home
Address	Work
	Cell
	Pager
Birthday	Fax
E-Mail	

Name		Home	
Address		Work	
		Cell	
		Pager	
Birthday		Fax	
E-Mail			

Name		Home	
Address		Work	
		Cell	
		Pager	
Birthday		Fax	
E-Mail			

Name		Home	
Address		Work	
		Cell	
		Pager	
Birthday		Fax	
E-Mail			

Name		Home	
Address		Work	
		Cell	
		Pager	
Birthday		Fax	
E-Mail			

Name		Home	
Address		Work	
		Cell	
		Pager	
Birthday		Fax	
E-Mail			

Name		Home	
Address		Work	
		Cell	
		Pager	
Birthday		Fax	
E-Mail			

ST

Name	Home
Address	Work
	Cell
	Pager
Birthday	Fax
E-Mail	

Name	Home
Address	Work
	Cell
	Pager
Birthday	Fax
E-Mail	

Name	Home
Address	Work
	Cell
	Pager
Birthday	Fax
E-Mail	

Name	Home
Address	Work
	Cell
	Pager
Birthday	Fax
E-Mail	

Name	Home
Address	Work
	Cell
	Pager
Birthday	Fax
E-Mail	

Name	Home
Address	Work
	Cell
	Pager
Birthday	Fax
E-Mail	

Name	Home
Address	Work
	Cell
	Pager
Birthday	Fax
E-Mail	

Name	Home
Address	Work
	Cell
	Pager
Birthday	Fax
E-Mail	

Name	Home
Address	Work
	Cell
	Pager
Birthday	Fax
E-Mail	

Name	Home
Address	Work
	Cell
	Pager
Birthday	Fax
E-Mail	

Name	Home
Address	Work
	Cell
	Pager
Birthday	Fax
E-Mail	

Name	Home
Address	Work
	Cell
	Pager
Birthday	Fax
E-Mail	

ST

Name	Home
Address	Work
	Cell
	Pager
Birthday	Fax
E-Mail	

Name	Home
Address	Work
	Cell
	Pager
Birthday	Fax
E-Mail	

Name	Home
Address	Work
	Cell
	Pager
Birthday	Fax
E-Mail	

Name	Home
Address	Work
	Cell
	Pager
Birthday	Fax
E-Mail	

Name	Home
Address	Work
	Cell
	Pager
Birthday	Fax
E-Mail	

Name	Home
Address	Work
	Cell
	Pager
Birthday	Fax
E-Mail	

ST

Name	Home
Address	Work
	Cell
	Pager
Birthday	Fax
E-Mail	

Name	Home
Address	Work
	Cell
	Pager
Birthday	Fax
E-Mail	

Name	Home
Address	Work
	Cell
	Pager
Birthday	Fax
E-Mail	

Name	Home
Address	Work
	Cell
	Pager
Birthday	Fax
E-Mail	

Name	Home
Address	Work
	Cell
	Pager
Birthday	Fax
E-Mail	

Name	Home
Address	Work
	Cell
	Pager
Birthday	Fax
E-Mail	

ST

Name	Home
Address	Work
	Cell
	Pager
Birthday	Fax
E-Mail	

Name	Home
Address	Work
	Cell
	Pager
Birthday	Fax
E-Mail	

Name	Home
Address	Work
	Cell
	Pager
Birthday	Fax
E-Mail	

Name	Home
Address	Work
	Cell
	Pager
Birthday	Fax
E-Mail	

Name	Home
Address	Work
	Cell
	Pager
Birthday	Fax
E-Mail	

Name	Home
Address	Work
	Cell
	Pager
Birthday	Fax
E-Mail	

And when the chief Shepherd shall appear, ye shall receive a crown of glory that fadeth not away.

1 Peter 5:4

Thomas Kinkade

u
v

Name	Home
Address	Work
	Cell
	Pager
Birthday	Fax
E-Mail	

Name	Home
Address	Work
	Cell
	Pager
Birthday	Fax
E-Mail	

Name	Home
Address	Work
	Cell
	Pager
Birthday	Fax
E-Mail	

Name	Home
Address	Work
	Cell
	Pager
Birthday	Fax
E-Mail	

Name	Home
Address	Work
	Cell
	Pager
Birthday	Fax
E-Mail	

Name	Home
Address	Work
	Cell
	Pager
Birthday	Fax
E-Mail	

UV

Name	Home
Address	Work
	Cell
	Pager
Birthday	Fax
E-Mail	

Name	Home
Address	Work
	Cell
	Pager
Birthday	Fax
E-Mail	

Name	Home
Address	Work
	Cell
	Pager
Birthday	Fax
E-Mail	

Name	Home
Address	Work
	Cell
	Pager
Birthday	Fax
E-Mail	

Name	Home
Address	Work
	Cell
	Pager
Birthday	Fax
E-Mail	

Name	Home
Address	Work
	Cell
	Pager
Birthday	Fax
E-Mail	

Name	Home
Address	Work
	Cell
	Pager
Birthday	Fax
E-Mail	

Name	Home
Address	Work
	Cell
	Pager
Birthday	Fax
E-Mail	

Name	Home
Address	Work
	Cell
	Pager
Birthday	Fax
E-Mail	

Name	Home
Address	Work
	Cell
	Pager
Birthday	Fax
E-Mail	

Name	Home
Address	Work
	Cell
	Pager
Birthday	Fax
E-Mail	

Name	Home
Address	Work
	Cell
	Pager
Birthday	Fax
E-Mail	

UV

Name	Home
Address	Work
	Cell
	Pager
Birthday	Fax
E-Mail	

Name	Home
Address	Work
	Cell
	Pager
Birthday	Fax
E-Mail	

Name	Home
Address	Work
	Cell
	Pager
Birthday	Fax
E-Mail	

Name	Home
Address	Work
	Cell
	Pager
Birthday	Fax
E-Mail	

Name	Home
Address	Work
	Cell
	Pager
Birthday	Fax
E-Mail	

Name	Home
Address	Work
	Cell
	Pager
Birthday	Fax
E-Mail	

UV

Name	Home
Address	Work
	Cell
	Pager
Birthday	Fax
E-Mail	

Name	Home
Address	Work
	Cell
	Pager
Birthday	Fax
E-Mail	

Name	Home
Address	Work
	Cell
	Pager
Birthday	Fax
E-Mail	

Name	Home
Address	Work
	Cell
	Pager
Birthday	Fax
E-Mail	

Name	Home
Address	Work
	Cell
	Pager
Birthday	Fax
E-Mail	

Name	Home
Address	Work
	Cell
	Pager
Birthday	Fax
E-Mail	

UV

Name	Home
Address	Work
	Cell
	Pager
Birthday	Fax
E-Mail	

Name	Home
Address	Work
	Cell
	Pager
Birthday	Fax
E-Mail	

Name	Home
Address	Work
	Cell
	Pager
Birthday	Fax
E-Mail	

Name	Home
Address	Work
	Cell
	Pager
Birthday	Fax
E-Mail	

Name	Home
Address	Work
	Cell
	Pager
Birthday	Fax
E-Mail	

Name	Home
Address	Work
	Cell
	Pager
Birthday	Fax
E-Mail	

Name	Home
Address	Work
	Cell
	Pager
Birthday	Fax
E-Mail	

Name	Home
Address	Work
	Cell
	Pager
Birthday	Fax
E-Mail	

Name	Home
Address	Work
	Cell
	Pager
Birthday	Fax
E-Mail	

Name	Home
Address	Work
	Cell
	Pager
Birthday	Fax
E-Mail	

Name	Home
Address	Work
	Cell
	Pager
Birthday	Fax
E-Mail	

Name	Home
Address	Work
	Cell
	Pager
Birthday	Fax
E-Mail	

UV

Name	Home
Address	Work
	Cell
	Pager
Birthday	Fax
E-Mail	

Name	Home
Address	Work
	Cell
	Pager
Birthday	Fax
E-Mail	

Name	Home
Address	Work
	Cell
	Pager
Birthday	Fax
E-Mail	

Name	Home
Address	Work
	Cell
	Pager
Birthday	Fax
E-Mail	

Name	Home
Address	Work
	Cell
	Pager
Birthday	Fax
E-Mail	

Name	Home
Address	Work
	Cell
	Pager
Birthday	Fax
E-Mail	

Heaven and earth shall pass away; but my words shall not pass away.

Luke 21:33

Thomas Kinkade

W
X

Name _____ Home _____
Address _____ Work _____
                              Cell _____
                              Pager _____
Birthday _____ Fax _____
E-Mail _____

Name _____ Home _____
Address _____ Work _____
                              Cell _____
                              Pager _____
Birthday _____ Fax _____
E-Mail _____

Name _____ Home _____
Address _____ Work _____
                              Cell _____
                              Pager _____
Birthday _____ Fax _____
E-Mail _____

Name _____ Home _____
Address _____ Work _____
                              Cell _____
                              Pager _____
Birthday _____ Fax _____
E-Mail _____

Name _____ Home _____
Address _____ Work _____
                              Cell _____
                              Pager _____
Birthday _____ Fax _____
E-Mail _____

Name _____ Home _____
Address _____ Work _____
                              Cell _____
                              Pager _____
Birthday _____ Fax _____
E-Mail _____

Name	Home
Address	Work
	Cell
	Pager
Birthday	Fax
E-Mail	

Name	Home
Address	Work
	Cell
	Pager
Birthday	Fax
E-Mail	

Name	Home
Address	Work
	Cell
	Pager
Birthday	Fax
E-Mail	

Name	Home
Address	Work
	Cell
	Pager
Birthday	Fax
E-Mail	

Name	Home
Address	Work
	Cell
	Pager
Birthday	Fax
E-Mail	

Name	Home
Address	Work
	Cell
	Pager
Birthday	Fax
E-Mail	

Name	Home
Address	Work
	Cell
	Pager
Birthday	Fax
E-Mail	

Name	Home
Address	Work
	Cell
	Pager
Birthday	Fax
E-Mail	

Name	Home
Address	Work
	Cell
	Pager
Birthday	Fax
E-Mail	

Name	Home
Address	Work
	Cell
	Pager
Birthday	Fax
E-Mail	

Name	Home
Address	Work
	Cell
	Pager
Birthday	Fax
E-Mail	

Name	Home
Address	Work
	Cell
	Pager
Birthday	Fax
E-Mail	

Name	Home
Address	Work
	Cell
	Pager
Birthday	Fax
E-Mail	

Name	Home
Address	Work
	Cell
	Pager
Birthday	Fax
E-Mail	

Name	Home
Address	Work
	Cell
	Pager
Birthday	Fax
E-Mail	

Name	Home
Address	Work
	Cell
	Pager
Birthday	Fax
E-Mail	

Name	Home
Address	Work
	Cell
	Pager
Birthday	Fax
E-Mail	

Name	Home
Address	Work
	Cell
	Pager
Birthday	Fax
E-Mail	

Name	Home
Address	Work
	Cell
	Pager
Birthday	Fax
E-Mail	

Name	Home
Address	Work
	Cell
	Pager
Birthday	Fax
E-Mail	

Name	Home
Address	Work
	Cell
	Pager
Birthday	Fax
E-Mail	

Name	Home
Address	Work
	Cell
	Pager
Birthday	Fax
E-Mail	

Name	Home
Address	Work
	Cell
	Pager
Birthday	Fax
E-Mail	

Name	Home
Address	Work
	Cell
	Pager
Birthday	Fax
E-Mail	

WX

Name	Home
Address	Work
	Cell
	Pager
Birthday	Fax
E-Mail	

Name	Home
Address	Work
	Cell
	Pager
Birthday	Fax
E-Mail	

Name	Home
Address	Work
	Cell
	Pager
Birthday	Fax
E-Mail	

Name	Home
Address	Work
	Cell
	Pager
Birthday	Fax
E-Mail	

Name	Home
Address	Work
	Cell
	Pager
Birthday	Fax
E-Mail	

Name	Home
Address	Work
	Cell
	Pager
Birthday	Fax
E-Mail	

Name	Home
Address	Work
	Cell
	Pager
Birthday	Fax
E-Mail	

Name	Home
Address	Work
	Cell
	Pager
Birthday	Fax
E-Mail	

Name	Home
Address	Work
	Cell
	Pager
Birthday	Fax
E-Mail	

Name	Home
Address	Work
	Cell
	Pager
Birthday	Fax
E-Mail	

Name	Home
Address	Work
	Cell
	Pager
Birthday	Fax
E-Mail	

Name	Home
Address	Work
	Cell
	Pager
Birthday	Fax
E-Mail	

WX

Name	Home
Address	Work
	Cell
	Pager
Birthday	Fax
E-Mail	

Name	Home
Address	Work
	Cell
	Pager
Birthday	Fax
E-Mail	

Name	Home
Address	Work
	Cell
	Pager
Birthday	Fax
E-Mail	

Name	Home
Address	Work
	Cell
	Pager
Birthday	Fax
E-Mail	

Name	Home
Address	Work
	Cell
	Pager
Birthday	Fax
E-Mail	

Name	Home
Address	Work
	Cell
	Pager
Birthday	Fax
E-Mail	

Yea, I have loved thee ... with an everlasting love.

Jeremiah 31:3

Thomas Kinkade

Y
Z

Name	Home
Address	Work
	Cell
	Pager
Birthday	Fax
E-Mail	

Name	Home
Address	Work
	Cell
	Pager
Birthday	Fax
E-Mail	

Name	Home
Address	Work
	Cell
	Pager
Birthday	Fax
E-Mail	

Name	Home
Address	Work
	Cell
	Pager
Birthday	Fax
E-Mail	

Name	Home
Address	Work
	Cell
	Pager
Birthday	Fax
E-Mail	

Name	Home
Address	Work
	Cell
	Pager
Birthday	Fax
E-Mail	

YZ

Name	Home
Address	Work
	Cell
	Pager
Birthday	Fax
E-Mail	

Name	Home
Address	Work
	Cell
	Pager
Birthday	Fax
E-Mail	

Name	Home
Address	Work
	Cell
	Pager
Birthday	Fax
E-Mail	

Name	Home
Address	Work
	Cell
	Pager
Birthday	Fax
E-Mail	

Name	Home
Address	Work
	Cell
	Pager
Birthday	Fax
E-Mail	

Name	Home
Address	Work
	Cell
	Pager
Birthday	Fax
E-Mail	

Name	Home
Address	Work
	Cell
	Pager
Birthday	Fax
E-Mail	

Name	Home
Address	Work
	Cell
	Pager
Birthday	Fax
E-Mail	

Name	Home
Address	Work
	Cell
	Pager
Birthday	Fax
E-Mail	

Name	Home
Address	Work
	Cell
	Pager
Birthday	Fax
E-Mail	

Name	Home
Address	Work
	Cell
	Pager
Birthday	Fax
E-Mail	

Name	Home
Address	Work
	Cell
	Pager
Birthday	Fax
E-Mail	

YZ

Name	Home
Address	Work
	Cell
	Pager
Birthday	Fax
E-Mail	

Name	Home
Address	Work
	Cell
	Pager
Birthday	Fax
E-Mail	

Name	Home
Address	Work
	Cell
	Pager
Birthday	Fax
E-Mail	

Name	Home
Address	Work
	Cell
	Pager
Birthday	Fax
E-Mail	

Name	Home
Address	Work
	Cell
	Pager
Birthday	Fax
E-Mail	

Name	Home
Address	Work
	Cell
	Pager
Birthday	Fax
E-Mail	

Name	Home
Address	Work
	Cell
	Pager
Birthday	Fax
E-Mail	

Name	Home
Address	Work
	Cell
	Pager
Birthday	Fax
E-Mail	

Name	Home
Address	Work
	Cell
	Pager
Birthday	Fax
E-Mail	

Name	Home
Address	Work
	Cell
	Pager
Birthday	Fax
E-Mail	

Name	Home
Address	Work
	Cell
	Pager
Birthday	Fax
E-Mail	

Name	Home
Address	Work
	Cell
	Pager
Birthday	Fax
E-Mail	

YZ

Name	Home
Address	Work
	Cell
	Pager
Birthday	Fax
E-Mail	

Name	Home
Address	Work
	Cell
	Pager
Birthday	Fax
E-Mail	

Name	Home
Address	Work
	Cell
	Pager
Birthday	Fax
E-Mail	

Name	Home
Address	Work
	Cell
	Pager
Birthday	Fax
E-Mail	

Name	Home
Address	Work
	Cell
	Pager
Birthday	Fax
E-Mail	

Name	Home
Address	Work
	Cell
	Pager
Birthday	Fax
E-Mail	

Name	Home
Address	Work
	Cell
	Pager
Birthday	Fax
E-Mail	

Name	Home
Address	Work
	Cell
	Pager
Birthday	Fax
E-Mail	

Name	Home
Address	Work
	Cell
	Pager
Birthday	Fax
E-Mail	

Name	Home
Address	Work
	Cell
	Pager
Birthday	Fax
E-Mail	

Name	Home
Address	Work
	Cell
	Pager
Birthday	Fax
E-Mail	

Name	Home
Address	Work
	Cell
	Pager
Birthday	Fax
E-Mail	

Name	Home
Address	Work
	Cell
	Pager
Birthday	Fax
E-Mail	

Name	Home
Address	Work
	Cell
	Pager
Birthday	Fax
E-Mail	

Name	Home
Address	Work
	Cell
	Pager
Birthday	Fax
E-Mail	

Name	Home
Address	Work
	Cell
	Pager
Birthday	Fax
E-Mail	

Name	Home
Address	Work
	Cell
	Pager
Birthday	Fax
E-Mail	

Name	Home
Address	Work
	Cell
	Pager
Birthday	Fax
E-Mail	